RHYMES
without
REASON

PENELOPE BOURDILLON

By the same author

How God can Peel on Onion
A bun dance

with Marcia Gibson-Watt

The Four Graces
Hope in the Valley:
(A Companion in Times of Bereavement)

Copyright © 2022 by Penelope Bourdillon

Paperback: 978-1-63767-763-6
eBook: 978-1-63767-764-3
Hardcover: 978-1-63767-765-0
Library of Congress Control Number: 2022903371

All rights reserved. No part of this publication may be reproduced, distributed, or transmitted in any form or by any electronic or mechanical means, without the prior written permission of the publisher, except in the case of brief quotations embodied in critical reviews and certain other noncommercial uses permitted by copyright law.

This is a work of nonfiction.

Ordering Information:

BookTrail Agency
8838 Sleepy Hollow Rd.
Kansas City, MO 64114

Printed in the United States of America

TABLE OF CONTENTS

INTRODUCTION
1   WITH THE BENSONS IN CORFU
5   THE PRICES' PROGRESS
6   A GREAT TRIP TO AMSTERDAM
8   LINDRIDGE
10   VENICE
12   THE NUGENT FAMILY
14   THE PLAYGIRLS AT PLET
16   PRINCESS GRACE HOSPITAL
17   RUPERT AND THE BANK AT GILWERN
18   THE ALGARVE
21   ODE TO NEV AND THEA
22   MERRIMENT ON MULL
24   ODE TO SOPHIA
25   IN SPAIN WITH THE STODDARTS
28   TIMBO'S LIMERICKS
30   TURKISH DELIGHT
33   A ROSY TOUR
34   MRS. NEVERWELL
36   HERTFORD, HEREFORD AND HAMPSHIRE
38   CLARE AND MY FAVOURITE NEPHEW

40	MICKY TO THE RESCUE
42	WITH THE GURKHAS IN NEPAL
47	MY EIGHTIETH BIRTHDAY
50	COVID CHRISTMAS
53	WHAT A PAIR!
55	CHRISTMAS IN DEVON

INTRODUCTION

These writings do not pretend to be a book of well written poetry. It is pure and simply a random and disparate collection of doggerel that I scribbled on and off during the past twenty five years, after doing something that had been fun: sometimes it was my thank you letter.

What I have always enjoyed about my life is the variety; perhaps these snippets do not reflect this because I probably only wrote one or two a year; of course I have done a great many other things which are not depicted here. However I hope it will give you a little glimpse of fun, friends and frivolity.

However, life is not always filled with fun and games, but I still intend to enjoy myself as I gallop through my eighties! There are several dear friends who are not included here, so please don't be offended if you are one of them.

In some cases I shall write a short explanation explaining the incident or event if it is not obvious what the occasion was.

I would like to dedicate this book to my dear friend
David Williams
who did the little drawings on the first few pages.
I would love him to have illustrated the whole book,
but very sadly he died several years ago.
I owe so much to him because it was
through him that I found Jesus.

WITH THE BENSONS IN CORFU

The Roberts and the Bensons
Chose two jewels in the crown
On that glorious Corfu coastline
Well away from Corfu town.

With Albania to the east of us -
So near and yet remote,
Richard led a party there
In a far from A1 boat.

So there we were the eight of us.
The Fausetts and the Lowndes,
With a swimming pool to die for
And tennis in the grounds.

We only had to walk about
A minute to the sea.
The temperature was perfect,
E'en for whimpering me.

Krystina and the Captain
were so nifty with the boat
it didn't take the Admiral
to keep us all afloat.

It was quite the perfect setting,
With no waves or sandy beaches;
And Sarah's really scrumptious food,
Plus honey, grapes and peaches.

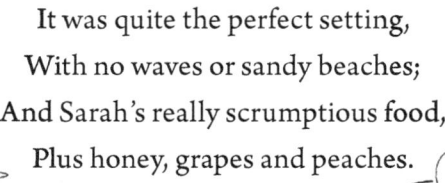

But disaster struck on Sunday morn,
Though it could have been **much worse**
And sixty stitches later
Anne returned without a nurse

Twas the only thing that marred the peace
As poor Tom drove back and forth
To the hospital in Corfu town
From our villa in the north.

Dear Anne was brave and cheery -
An example to us all.....
Then Julian met a jelly fish
And Mervyn had a fall.

While Cinna swam for miles,
And kept us all in fits,
Julian taught me how to crawl,
With those nasty breathing bits;

"Will you try a little harder"
(he cried) - "don't lift your head so high.
You look just like a porpoise
reaching for the sky."

There were dogs to take a-walking
In the soft refreshing breeze,
Where paths galore we did explore
Betwixt the olive trees.

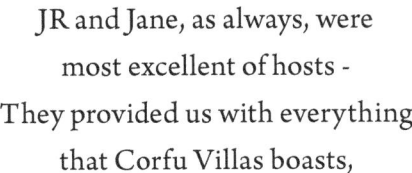

We had such fun, and laughs and jokes,
Though most were rather silly;
Hardly fit for college men
When the batsman was called Willy

JR and Jane, as always, were
most excellent of hosts -
They provided us with everything
that Corfu Villas boasts,

and more besides, like books and things -
You only had to ask
and "mozzie traps" and Floris soap,
just right for every task

It really was luxurious,
And so typical of Jane
to think of all the little things
Just purely for our gain.

With clerics' sons to right of us,
Archbishops (unknown) to left;
Without the Riou Bensons
We'd clearly be bereft.

How could we be so lucky
To have such dear kind friends?
And we were so very sad to leave
But all holidays must end.

Julian and Jane have been wonderful friends over the years, and I still love staying with them in their new home. They are incredibly generous and we have been on several glorious holidays in Corfu where they used to take a villa.

THE PRICES' PROGRESS

The Lees' charming house they decided to buy,
with a beautiful view right down to the Wye.
As they tried to move in, with their dogs and the cats
'Twas apparent there **were** some huge problems with bats.

They **thought** that they'd bought a nice house near a chapel,
but then there began the most fiercely fought battle ...
Batty people came down like the wolf on the fold
crying 'Bats must **not** be subjected to cold'.

The boiler room 'd be good, the B's dared to suggest,
not stopping to think of what they'd infest.
A suitable building was offered instead.
'You must build the wall higher' - are these B's off their head?

'What have we done to deserve this?' they ask,
as the Ministry men take them to task...
'So what shall we do?' they wail in fear -
'We **do** not want rabid night creatures in here'.

Just in case the Ministry folk think we're cheating,
we'd best build a belfry with good central heating.
With stuff from IKEA, and wall to wall mats,
and signpost it, saying **THIS WAY FOR ALL BATS**.

A GREAT TRIP TO AMSTERDAM

When we went with Willow to Amsterdam
We went on an aeroplane, boat and a tram.
No-one got lost, and we hadn't a care,
'cos whenever we wanted her Willow was there.
She looked after us all with our various needs
And rescued us from some terrible deeds.
Betty Watson gave her a horrible fright
When she stood in the street in the midst of the night!

NADFAS laid on the most wonderful guide:
"We all take a fancy to Nancy" we cried.
She talked of some subjects we may never have known,
And took us to things we were thrilled to be shown.
The great Rijksmuseum was a feast to behold,
And I loved the historical facts that she told.
She made it so interesting, right from the start,
And inspired us with treats of van Gogh and his art.

Of course we all held Rembrandt in awe,
But I don't think we realised quite what was in store:
His etchings and sketchings and engravings galore;
We just gazed at them hanging on ever-y floor.
Nancy took us all round and she talked as she walked
As if a huge treasure trove she had uncorked.
First the Jewish Museum, and then the Town Hall,
And a church in a house - we savoured them all.

Then through the Red Light District we actually strolled,
And learned that the system's quite strictly controlled.
Oh yes - we went on a bus with a driver named Carla -
She was tiny and blonde, but she made no palaver:
Though the bus was so long and the streets were so narrow,
Her precision was almost like that of an arrow.
Thus we carefully avoided the sex and the drugs!
Though we knew Amsterdam is full of those thugs.

We loved the boat trip up and down the canals
And had such good laughs with all of our pals;
We'd never have managed it all on our own;
Just think of the things we might never have known.
Congrats to NADFAS for gath'ring us together -
There was only one grumble, and that was the weather.
Thank you dear Willow - you showed us such beauty .
And looked after us well - and way beyond duty.

LINDRIDGE

I am extremely fortunate to have some really special friends who have been so good to me since my husband died. The Andrewes are such, and this page is dedicated to them, with thanks for many years of wonderful friendship. I often stay at their beautiful house which I call my second home. Some years ago Bill decided to make a rill...

Oh! What a thrill
To see the great rill,
For which Bill took his quill to pay the fat bill.

As the water doth spill
Over said rill
There is never so much as a waste or a spill.

Any Jack and his Jill
Can come take their fill:
No need to climb that treacherous hill.

Let us hope that no ill
E'er befalls the fine rill -
That would certainly be a most bitter pill.

Many gardeners would kill
To have such a rill:
It adds to the place a most elegant 'frill'.

If you don't have a mill,
Or a rill, in fact nil,
You just have to rely on your gardening skill.

So Bill must be thrilled with his beautiful rill
And now he must wait for the gates on the hill.

Bill's wife is always called Boo. Some years ago she arranged a ladies' outing to a London theatre, after having lunch at the Royal Academy. I can't remember what she had in her bag, but it did cause a bit of bother having to be deposited in the cloakrooms along our way.

BOO'S COTERIE

I was queueing for the Cloakroom, so I could park Boo's plastic bag;
(When we left the Royal Academy I even had the tag).
Then Boo's splendid little Coterie walked to St. Martin's Lane,
where she had to disappear to drop said bag again…

I wonder - did she go to the COATERY or HATTERY?
Thank God we had no use for a DOGGERY or CATTERY.
If we'd had a scooter, would it go into a SCOOTERY?
But that day we had a need for a special sort of
BOO-TERY

VENICE

Last month we went to Venice with Gillie as our leader,
And Sarah was the expert, and goodness, did we need her!

She met us at the Airport, and all was very well;
We sped off in a motor boat right up to our hotel.

She shared with us her favourite things, and was a fount of knowledge,
Which was wonderful for those of us who'd never been to College.

We had drinks within a merchant's house, and visited palazzas
And wound our ways down alleyways, and through glorious piazzas.

We learned of the Evangelists: St. Mark with winged li-on,
St Matthew and the angel, with the Eagle for St. John.

And then there were the saints..... St. Peter had his keys,
And mystical Madonnas with the Babe upon their knees.

Poor Sebastian was depicted with those arrows well embedded,
Though he didn't meet his death 'til he was finally beheaded.

We heard about the healing saints, but they hardly scan or rhyme:
And then there were the "doctors": like Jerome and Augustine.

Franciscans and Dominicans in rivalry displayed
Their churches, housing wondrous art, the pilgrims to persuade.

And we doted on Carpaccio, Veronese, and the rest....
Too numerous to name, but for us Bellini was the best.

Then we took a vaporetta and went up the Grand Canal
Past th' Rialto, the Pescaria to the Railway Terminal.

St. Mark's was unsurpassable - I think you'll all agree.
Everybody has their favourite, but that's the one for me.

Mervyn thought Torcello was the jewel in the crown
And lunch at Devil's Bridge was of particular renown.

I could go on for longer, but I mustn't be a bore,
But we have not even touched upon the great St. Theodore.

This comes with gratitude and praise, and our thanks to you and yours
And all the very best to those well-known Miss(en)den Tours.

THE NUGENT FAMILY

I used to spend quite a lot of time in Lambourn with two very special friends, John and Pepe Nugent, before they went to Ireland to run the family home, Ballinlough. They are one of my favourite families and we were therefore extremely sad not to be able to get over there for their son Nick's wedding to Alice. We sent them this rather silly message on the day; he is well known in the Racing world, which explains the jargon - for the uninitiated.

> Now the 'chasing season is over, and you are firmly on the flat -
> there will be the odd hurdle, but we know you'll cope with that.
> May the ground be always firm, and the going always good …
> we are sad we can't be with you; we do so wish we could.
> But we're pleased you picked the winner for the 'race' that matters most,
> and this brings our best love, and congratulations - that's our toast.

Happily we **were** able to go to my Goddaughter Grania's wonderful wedding in the Castle which was like a fairy tale, on a glorious autumn day. Pepe gave an extremely good talk which made the Service very special.

> Because we love the Nugents so, we flew across the water
> for a most auspicious day: the marriage of their daughter.
>
> We know the Irish weather could have put us to the test,
> but Ballinlough was looking at its very, very best
>
> with lights upon the lake, and the garden so well tended,
> in resplendent autumn colours – just as you'd intended.

'twas lucky, was it not, that we didn't get a wetting?
And the drawing room and the dining room made such a perfect setting.

The 'Sir' looked justly proud with his daughter on his arm;
with so many friends around her, and the atmosphere was calm.

I know that the Almighty was not invited by the Bride,
but I have a funny sort of feeling He was right there by her side.

After all, we ask that He might use our hearts, our ears, and lips,
and that's exactly what He did through dear and good, brave Peps:

As the Bride's mama got up to give her excellent address
I do most fervently believe that His longing was to bless.

And then there was the dancing in the wonderful marquee,
with Nick's great speech so funny, as only he can be.

Delicious food and drink - from Guinness to Champagne,
and 'twas good to see dear Betty back upon her feet again,

And Gordon at the ready to meet anyone's requests,
having danced the night away like the other happy guests.

Fierce posh they were – and weren't we all! But what I really want to say:
good health, good luck, and happiness – not just on their wedding day.

It surely is a week-end we always shall remember:
Stu and Grania's wedding, the twenty ninth September.

THE PLAYGIRLS AT PLET

Our lovely friends at Plettenberg had quite the nicest place:
The architect, it must be said, must have been an ace.

It was all on different levels, with a stunning view from each,
perched up high above the bay with little steps down to the beach.

We had a puncture near East London. The Vicar kindly rescued us;
But it was in bandit country where there would never be a bus!

Poor Mervyn had been poorly, and looked whiter than a sheet;
but he soon began to gather strength with what Lindy gave us all to eat.

We had de-elicious fruit - and fresh fish from the sea,
and with such enormous dinners there was never room for tea.

We ate and laughed and walked and swam, but there was another feature:
I very nearly learned to surf, with Lindy as my teacher.

Occasionally I could get it right, and roared along in style.
but other times were hopeless - I was just an **un**-guided missile!

Susan and I imagined we were dolphins in the ocean,
but all we really managed was to cause a slight commotion.

The real dolphins jumped and played just below us in the Bay;
Susan could just see them, as on her bed she lay.

We had lunch at Lookout Bay, and walked home without a rush:
We had to get Aunt Diney back, to her pallet and her brush.

Then there were the shops at Plet, and it really was a pleasure
    to go with Sue and Lindy - because we were all at leisure.

    I do hope, with the Dixorit and all the other pills,
        that Dave won't have a migraine, or any other ills.

Did you ever get to Knysna? Did you find the pharmacist?
    What about the 'Bristol Cocktail'? I hope he could assist.

Well, you dear kind generous people, I must stop this Tommy rot
    'cause all we really want to do is thank you both … **a lot.**

Lindy was so supportive when Mervyn was dying, and now she has her own problems with her beloved David's illness.

PRINCESS GRACE HOSPITAL

If you have to spend a month in hospital, which I did some time ago, this is a great place to be. I was so well looked after.

A is for ANGUISH which brings us here when we're ill.
B is for BUPA who we hope pays the bill!
C is for CHRISTINE and COMFORT, COMPASSION and CARE.
D is for DONNA, with wisdom to share.
E is for Ebrahim who fixes our mood.
F is for FRANCIS and the de-elicious food.
G is for GLENDA; and Princess GRACE and her beauty.
H is for He (and she) who all do their duty.
I's for INDIVIDUALS and the grace that they show.
J is for Jennifer, Justin and Jo.
K is Key: the most brilliant physician and
L is for Dr. LIBBY who is a magician.
M is MADDY from India: efficient and bright.
Nancy and Nike are the stars of the Night.
Oh! I am lucky to be here; I really know that.
P is for PILLS and POTIONS and wonderful PAT.
Q is the letter that stumps me completely.
R is the rest that heals one so sweetly and
S is for sleep that has been such a hitch.
T is for tea at the press of a switch.
U 's to unburden all we don't need,
Vanishing now with quite reasonable speed.
We are so grateful for all that you do ... never avoiding the
Xtra mile or two.
You are all angels: thanks for being so kind.
Z is must be the very best place one could find.

RUPERT AND THE BANK AT GILWERN

You did it. You planned it. You brought all the plants.
You then put them into all the right places.
All I want now is to sing and to dance
Ev'ry time I look at their bright shining faces.

We made the stone bolsters; you saw the big *pitcher;*
You sculpted the bank - and moved tons of soil;
You got us all working. It's lucky we're *fit 'ere!*
It was worth every moment of back breaking toil.

They've been well watered in by torrents of rain,
So let's hope through the winter that they will survive;
And then in the spring when you come back again
You will see that your dear little 'children' still thrive.

You were so good to turn and finish the task.
esp. with your wedding so quickly approaching,
I felt it really was too much to ask
I was worried that Alice would think
(the Welsh job) was encroaching.

So thank you dear Rupert for your talent and vigour;
I'm so pleased and so grateful for all you have done.
Don't be late for your wedding ('tis not de rigeur).
Then off on your 'moon, and see lots of sun.

Rupert Rankin planned the upper bank for me at Gilwern. Having bought all the plants which he drove down in his mother's pig trailer, he then helped me plant them - all 580 of them.

THE ALGARVE

Quite a lot of poetic licence is needed with this one. Extra lines put in at random! and I tend to put brackets round a word, in the interest of scanning.

I had a very jolly holiday with very dear friends in Portugal, which was particularly poignant the year after my husband had died. My swimming is particularly bad, which you should have picked up already!

I went to the Algarve to stay with the Bennetts;
The Dyers were there, and the hours flew like minutes.
We behaved like teenagers who hadn't a care
And prob'ly embarrassed 'most everyone there.

Too many cooks **can** spoil the broth,
But we all worked together, and ne'er was there wrath;
Val at the barbie meant Dourado supreme,
(Otherwise known as Goldheaded Bream)
And his fresh orange juice was more than a dream.

There was Holiday Sauce with prawns of course,
And fresh fish to die for, called Basil;
And olives, tomatoes, avocadoes, potatoes,
And nothing was burned to a frazzle.

We swam in th' Atlantic; the excitement was frantic
After mounds of sardines at Maria's.
We drank too much by far, think of Jane's 'Sang-ree-aa',
At the other beach bar named Ju-lee-a's.

Mike and I were the pigs who loved soaking the figs
In a marinade made from white wine;
And woe betide Jane as she cleared up again,
If she tried to throw **them** in the bin.

After dinner one night MaryAnn went to swim –
Did she really think it was the best way to slim?
And then I joined in, and felt a right fool
When I bumped my thick head on the end of the pool.

But worse was to come, as we made such a noise
And we couldn't blame any of the boys.
The people upstairs said, "You terrible guys",
So next day we went up to apologise.

Now let's look at the tests that were set for the guests:
Mango pud, but that just had to be slung out;
Presentation of food, sometimes horribly rude
With dear Basil displayed with his tongue out.

The gals let their hair down, and took off their glasses
And got up early to practise for **my** swimming classes (!)
Competition was fierce, which could have meant tears
(Though they had been shed over lost Boarding passes).
But there never was doubt in anyone's eyes
When MaryAnn walked off with the Limerick prize.

We walked over the Bridge at the Quinta do Lago,
Then drove down the coast through the Vale do Lobo.
We shopped till we dropped at the Mini Mercado,
Which was just down the steps at the Villa do Logo.

So now I must say, in a roundabout way,
Huge thanks to those wonderful B's
For the laughter and fun, and high jinks in the sun,
And for putting us all at our ease.

So, Four Seasons, farewell - it really was swell -
And *Obligata* dear friends for a fabulous time.
I shall now return home with such tales to tell …
And send apologies for such a ludicrous rhyme.

ODE TO NEV AND THEA

Neville is another very special friend who has been so helpful in many and varied ways since Mervyn died. His beloved wife Thea has not been at all well for some time, which is very sad for him.

This should be sung to the tune of Oh! Mr. Porter, whatever shall I do?
I wanted to go to Birmingham, but you took me on to Crewe.

Oh! Dr. Neville, whatever should I do
If I didn't have such a lovely friend to talk to as I do:
From enduring Powers of Attorney, and how many *mgs* to take
To insurance and insomnia, and the things we love to hate.

Then there is clever and wondrous Thea without whom I can't manage at all
When it comes to deciding on curtains and what colours to go on the wall.
Our trip to Painswick was a huge triumph (and what a treat to see Tim!)
And then the Rococo Garden was a bonus just thrown in.

You've been so very good to me, especially since Mervyn died.
I'd never have survived on my own, however hard I tried.
Thank you for picking me up sometimes when things were really bad;
It always is such fun with you, and I quite forget to feel sad.

MERRIMENT ON MULL

I went off to stay on the Isle of Mull:
There was never a moment you'd ever call dull.

At Grasspoint we squabbled one night on the floor
"Take two" someone cried – just when I was going to score!

Then next day we went to the Hall at Craignure
And bedecked it with bunting and ribbons galore.

Then back to the house for much food and more booze;
We all tore around; there was no time to lose.

Isla kept cooking delectable grub:
Quite plainly no need to go to the pub.

Then the boat was pushed out at Torosay Castle,
Where all the best friends would arrive with a parcel.

What was the cause for such preparation?
There was clearly to be a Big Celebration …

Why such an auspicious and memorable day?
Of course! it was …

RUPERT DE KLEE'S IMPORTANT BIRTHDAY

The barbecue was ready; the boys had done the wood;
But Charlotte started panicking: would we run out of food?

We counted up to fifty three, and then there were some more.
Then some other families. Help! Could it be ninety four?

Yesterday they caught a crab – and one lobster in the pot,
But without a blooming miracle, that would never feed this lot.

I am quite sure that none went hungry, though we all had quite a thirst.
I did, having raced through the Reel of th' Fifty First.

I whirled around the floor with kind men I met by chance,
And even quite enjoyed the Canadian Barn Dance.

But now I have to say Goodbye and wend my way down south
With so many happy memories to tell my friends about.

Dear Lara and Kyle and Ivan and Jo,
You've all been so kind, but it's time to go.

Rupert and Charlotte, you're such wonderful cousins.
May the Lord keep you safe, and send blessings in dozens.

Thank you so much, and with love to you all, from
'Rent-a-Granny'

I love my trips to Mull with Richard my wonderful Godson, as well as Rupert and Charlotte. They are all such good friends to me.

ODE TO SOPHIA

There once was a lady from Senny
Whose talents were varied and many:
In music sh' excelled
'Speshly Baroque' (she yelled)
But now I've no room to tell any …

Of her other gifts which include particularly:

Prayer Warrior extraordinaire

Present give sublime

Horse lover supreme

Librarian (purveyor of books) wondrous

Hostess magnifique
and
Giver of time genereuse.

Sophia is a serious musician, having played her baroque oboe all over the world. I am learning to play the flute, but not at all well! She was trying to explain to me how to breathe properly …

I have always breathed in through my nose,
And natur-ally my shoulders arose.
But Sophia says (and she knows) That I must
start to breathe through my TOES.

She and her husband David have been very kind and I sometimes stay there before we both go to the most wonderful Bible Study group near them once a month.

IN SPAIN WITH THE STODDARTS

The two Stoddart brothers, now sadly both dead, were wonderful friends to me for well over sixty years. Dave's wife Jane very kindly asked me to join them in Spain for a week where we had a wonderful time. Pete is always known as Fred, and his wife as Mable.

In the mountains of Spain, where ne'er does it rain;
I've just been to stay for a week.
We did have a phone 'ere - at the Casa Antonia -
but I never had reason to speak.

I flew out with the Stods, and we stayed with the Stods
… Jane keeps the most wonderful table.
And Dave plied us with drink 'til we no longer could think:
that goes for me - **and** Fred and Mable.

For the holiday mood and such scrumptious food
completely overtook us (all five);
We ate and we drank and we swam 'til we sank.
It was good to be there - and alive.

Fred hired a car 'cos the Airport was far,
and he drove me along, very kindly.
The car ran on diesel. He wanted to please all,
but had filled it with petrol, quite blindly.

It just would not start - not even a spark
on one of the back streets of Gaucine.
What to do next was somewhat complex,
because Crown Hire was not to be seen.

You'd not want to alter that sight of Gibraltar,
with such long distant views to be seen:
the African coast, e'en Libya (almost) and
Fred said, 'that's where I served the Queen'.

Amidst all the laughter we were so well looked after:
Antonia cleared up for us all.
There was never a mess, nor a moment of stress
for Glyn was always on call.

Once to Ronda we flew, stopping to view
at a glorious spot called a Mirador.
The breakfast enormous, but only for four of us
at the posh place that was once a Parador.

We drank with Diana at her very fine 'manor',
and lunched with the Fenwicks at home.
We shopped 'til we dropped, at the Bullring we stopped,
and I never once felt on my own.

So we read and we laughed, and continued to quaff:
Manzilla and wine did we booze.
Dave & Jane you can boast: you're the hosts with the most
and deserve the very top Michelin Rouge.

But hols have to have ends, and so, you dear friends,
it's time to go home - and I have to say
for my days in the sun and all the good fun -
huge thanks for my GREAT holi-day.

TIMBO'S LIMERICKS

This is for a very special friend who got married the day after us and we have had a great deal of fun together during the past sixty years, and still do. We decided that we would celebrate our Golden Weddings even though our husbands were dead, and we had a wonderful trip round the Islands off the West coast of Scotland.

Her husband Philip once gave me a book of Limericks, some of which I refer to below...

> Please tell that young man in his castle
> not to do up any more parcels.

> I'm so glad I don't live on the coast –
> 'cos I'd never dare open my post.

> But it's so nice the plumber still comes
> to my neighbour who needs one who plumbs.

> Now, I don't want to fall off his ladder
> while Titian is mixing his madder.

> I am quite happy in my pagoda
> although it's so far from Baroda.

> Do you know the one about Coles Hill
> when the poor lady sat on a mole's hill?

I shall end up with a nice clean one.

> There was a young man from Nepal
> who went to a fancy dress ball.
> He thought that he'd risk it
> and go as a biscuit
> and a dog ate him up in the hall.

TURKISH DELIGHT

Off we went to Turkey with Stuart Bell and Pru,
with such a lot to learn about, and much to see and do.

The group were fun: we saw the sun; we went to Istanbul:
majestic on the Bosporus, mysterious ... and beautiful.

The Blue Mosque stood supreme in its misty blue/gray aura,
But was almost surpassed by St Saviour's (that's in Chora).

Dear Taner was a brilliant guide, and told us copious facts,
and Stuart read from Revelation, Philippians, Luke and Acts.

We said Psalms, sang hymns and spiritual things, in diverse and sundry places and shared bread and wine at St. Polycarp's shrine, joined by folk from other places.

But my lasting memory will surely be of singing MAJESTY at Ephesus
and the stories told by saints of old - and the legacy they have left us.

The book of Revelation I've seldom dared to read before;
now, thanks to Stuart's exposition, I understand a little more.

We travelled many miles in the comfort of our coach
with Mehmut as our driver, with nothing to reproach.

We crossed the Dardanelles by ferry, and saw (the) Gallipoli Memorial.
I'd no idea, but it soon became clear, that Turkey's so arborial.

We learned of Anatolia and the customs of the Turkish;
of the Ottomans and Ataturk, and about the Whirling Dervish.

The flags all flew at half mast (there'd been disaster down the mine):
We drove very close to Soma, but there was not a single sign.

We wallowed in a Thermal Pool, and had a Turkish bath;
Then Marcia bought a Turkish Carpet - could've been a dangerous path!

We sped to Troy where, oh joy, we saw a Wooden Horse,
and we learned that the city was built on high: on nine levels - of course.

But 'twas about Paul's Seven Churches we'd really come to hear:
Smyrna, Thyatira; Philadelphia; Laodicea;

Up the cable car at Pergamum to see a wondrous site,
then a comfort stop, and a quick shop, just to keep Dorothy bright!

Ruined temples to Diana (Artemis in ancient Greek)
made me want the ancient columns to reassemble, then to speak

of Ancient Days in Bible times when Paul was busy preaching:
when people then seemed very keen, and flocked to hear his teaching.

John and Fay gave us each a white stone for our own:
Mine 'spoke' to me and said, quite simply: **STONE** ...

I asked God for a further 'word', (never sure of my discernment) ...
wondered if it really came from Him and, if so, what it meant;

It was really just a gently nudge, but I think He meant **'KEEP BUILDING'**-
out of doors and on the rock: not indoors - nor with gilding.

I shall take it as encouragement to build more steps and walls,
using local stone to create them - and even waterfalls?

So now, O Lord I pray that you will use Gilwern as your own
To spread the good news of the Gospel there, using me as well as stone.

A ROSY TOUR

I met up with Rosie at the Castell Deuddraeth
to explore some great wonders of mystery and myth.

We ate and drank at the Castell until we were quite sated,
then set forth to enjoy what Clough Williams Ellis had created:

Port Meirion spreads over a remarkable space:
the Italianate village in a beautiful place.

Then off to the island of Anglesey we sped,
again deliciously wined and watered and fed.

We only went there by special appointment,
and I can assure you 'twas no disappointment.

We met there the owner digging sludge from a pond,
assisted by a bloke of whom he was fond.

There were camellias, rhododendrons, azaleas galore
and geraniums, and other good plants by the score.

'Rosy Tours' are to be most highly commended -
I was bitterly sad when this one was ended.

What a marvellous tour dear Rosie you'd planned,
and we experienced simply the best of the land.

MRS. NEVERWELL

Years ago I spent a very happy skiing holiday with my son and his family. The three granddaughters (who call me Dare) started badly as it was their first time, and I thought I had lost my nerve having not skied for so long.

I was about to have a hip replacement, and the painkillers I took made me feel dizzy in that altitude. However, things got better, and we had a wonderful last day all skiing together so all our problems were forgotten.

> We all went to ski there in Val d'Isere
> including Mrs Neverwell (that's a.k.a. Dare);
> she got confused by the lifts, and fell off the 'chair'
> and never could find her own way - anywhere there.
>
> She hadn't put on skis for twenty nine years,
> and first day was o'ercome by terrible fears;
> Patrick was patient and relinquished his fun
> to take his old mother straight down a green run.
>
> The next day dawned bright, and nice runs did we find;
> this time it was Miranda's turn to be kind.
> She skied jolly well: not too fast nor too slow,
> and showed the mother-in-law just where to go.
>
> On Wednesday Patrick was really a wizard -
> and got Mum up to Solaise in a slight blizzard.
> She said she was dizzy and couldn't see straight,
> so he had to be patient and stand there and wait.

She could hardly get herself back down to the town!
Even though the telepherique took one right down.
You'd think even she would manage the bubble,
but she nearly got into some terrible trouble.

On Thursday she started whingeing again -
this time she had a mini migraine.
Isabel didn't feel too well either,
so they spent all that day convalescing together.

Caroline and Maxine saw to our extreme well being;
there was plenty to do as well as the skiing:
Backgammon, games, knitting; **and** we would sew,
then performed an amateur magic show.

But on Friday the old girl went on a journey;
up, up and over - all the way right to Le Fournet.
There were marvellous lifts: five, six, even seven,
leading through scenery quite fit for heaven.

She was up and away, enjoying every moment;
can there really not be a single lament?!
By this time even Flora was going for her life:
when she started she **did** have considerable strife.

For Miranda's birthday we had quite a feast,
and then we all five somehow managed the piste...
skied all day long with the girls on top form -
and even the Fog Horn (Rose) came for the morn.

Happy days!

HERTFORD, HEREFORD AND HAMPSHIRE

(with apologies to G.B.Shaw)

When I learned to sew in London, I met Veronica B-L;
she had a brother Richard, whom I got to know as well.

I first knew Cinna when we were at an awful school in **Herts**.
She always was good fun, and very, very good at art.

Then later on at Kiki Byrne - when we both went there to work -
but with Cinna's sense of humour we were inclined to shirk.

Richard lived in Limerston Street, and used to do the round
of friends in London's Culford Gardens where we worked, underground.

He then moved to **Hampshire**, and Cinna was in Glos.
These were sad and troubled years and over which we'll gloss.

But happier times at Haffield brought them further west
and for all of us who went there, it was the very best.

Now they are at Eyton where everything's just swell:
perhaps they could rename it - (*Dun Roamin'* would do well).

They've made a very special home: such trouble they did take,
with stunning views and parkland; woods, gardens, and a lake.

And their beautiful belongings and their quite exquisite taste ...
I'd like to have stayed longer but I was, as so often, in great haste.

It's good they're still near **Hereford** - which is just where they belong.
Let's hope the years they spend there will be peaceful, good and long.

Thank you both for such a long and happy friendship.

CLARE AND MY FAVOURITE NEPHEW

I have just stayed with the K-W's:
'twas a terrific weekend in November.
With Pete, Clare, Coco, Kitty and Isis -
and it's one that I'll always remember.

Clare and I had a heavenly ride:
we went up over dale and hill;
We walked, trotted, cantered - and galloped,
But then befell what could have been ill.

Her horse cast a shoe on the near fore;
and that might have been a disaster.
Charlotte came to our aid with the horsebox;
and she could not have come any faster.

So many excitements seemed to follow.
In that Tesla of Pete's (one of my favourite treats)
when we whizzed off at nought to 100,
to Petworth to buy lots of sweets.

We talked of our family forebears
Of whom they want to know more:
Both the good and the bad and dangerous -
and Aunt Betty sweeping the floor.

And Clare was delighted to hear
(and with glee they both held up their hands)
when they discovered, with utter surprise,
the Connection with the Kineton-Nosebands!

There was time to do the giant crossword,
and then they we sped off to the pub
where we drank and chatted and laughed
and ate some jolly good grub.

This doesn't seem to rhyme or scan much! but it was all such fun.

Thank you all for a very jolly time.

MICKY TO THE RESCUE
Gales and Tales

I stayed with a very old friend on my way up to Scotland. Time was short and I got stuck in traffic on the way, and she cleverly rearranged for her hairdresser to come and do my hair, which was a great help because I would not have time before my cousin's funeral.

I then mislaid my mobile phone, which was actually in the car. I went out to get it, and I cannot have shut the boot properly because during the night there was a mighty gale, and Micky found it wide open in the morning when she was walking her dogs. My clothes were soaking wet, but I had no idea of what had happened, so I was somewhat surprised to see them hanging up in her kitchen when I came down!

> Thank heavens for Micky when things got a bit tricky,
> as I set out on my travels from Wales.
> **What** a great friend, 'cos she put to an end
> all my problems and trials and wails!
>
> Though my ETA changed, she still managed t' arrange
> for dear Laura to sort out my hair.
> Then, I really must mention, she turned her attention
> to ABUNDANCE - with artistic flair.
>
> We chatted and laughed as her Rose we quaffed,
> and galloped down Memory Lane.
> In the morning came trouble, which would have been double
> but Micky came to the rescue again.

My clothes were all wet, and I wanted to set
off on my way to Kirkcudbright:
But Micky was there, with lots of hot air,
and got them all beautifully dry.

So off I went forth - on my long journey north
and I drove through bad storms, floods and gales.
Then my back tyre was flat - I could just cope with that
but I have some more terrible tales!

WITH THE GURKHAS IN NEPAL

Robin and Marcia Gibson-Watt have been very great friends for over half a century, and have seen me through thick and thin. Marcia is a professional artist, and we have done some books together. Geoffrey Ashley asked her if she would join his party to go out to Nepal to paint some of the celebrations to mark 200 years of 2nd King Edward VII's Own Goorkha Rifles (The Simoor Rifles). She kindly asked me to go with her as Robin didn't want to, and it is one of the happiest times I have spent, and there are so many amazing memories to look back on. I hope I captured a little of the spirit of the Nepalese in the following pages:

> Off we set, upon a jet, to join the Ashley's group;
> it took much preparation, and they kept us in the loop.
> 2 GR's Celebrations we had gone out to attend:
> Two hundred years of faithful service – and loyal to the end.

> The Gurkhas came down like the wolf on the fold,
> from the mountains they came - the old and the bold:
> with Yambahadur, Khana and Rambahadur too,
> all gathered to register for the Tattoo.

> We learned to say Namasté - that is their way of greeting;
> we bowed our heads with prayerful hands to all whom we were meeting.
> I loved the colours; the atmosphere; the religious toleration -
> 'twould be good if the affluent West would learn much from this Nation.

CANCELLATION IN KATHMANDU

For the first Durbar - hoorah! hoorah! we donned our finest clothes;
there was hot sun in the morning, then heav'n turned on its hose.
Wondrous things had been prepared, with bands, parades and staging.
But alas it had to be abandoned: a fierce and mighty storm was raging.

Though it dampened not our ardour, we were
soaked right through and through;
happily we had just begun, and there was much left to do.
Next day we made the journey - sev'n hours in a minibus
through the beauty of the foothills of the great Himala-y-a-s.

PARTIES AT POKHARA

There was a Luncheon Function when they fed three thousand people;
the unveiling of the (Me)morial Arch by Field Marshall Sir John Chappell.
Simoori Medals were presented, and we listened to the Band;
the Queen's Truncheon* was marched in - for which everyone would stand.

DURBAR DAY

Simoori Club Nepal, at Pokhara Exhibition Ground
was where the next event took place, and excitement did abound.
It was a most important day and this time nothing was delayed
at the Second Goorkhas' Two Hundredth Anniversary Parade.

To me the icing on the cake, and an unexpected treat,
was when we gathered in the dusk to watch them Sound Retreat.
The Brigade of Gurkhas Band and Pipes marched and played beside
the Nepalese Army Band - and they all took it in their **stride.

---

*   *The Truncheon is the equivalent of a Regiment's Colour, hence its huge importance.*
** *The unique double quick March adopted from the 60th Rifles after 1857.*

Huge and fascinating photographs along one end of the (Parade) ground
showed their exploits in far countries where their reputation does abound.
Depicting the history in vast pictorial form;
it was beautifully presented, and way beyond the norm.

There were dancing girls, whose skirts did swirl
with each graceful movement;
then some sang, and the mountains rang with music and emotion.
It was poignant and nostalgic, in a magnificent location,
for the great family of Goorkhas to host this last occasion.

We met signalmen and riflemen and several Gurkha Majors;
I tried to learn the Regiments and all their different stages:
i.e. the joining of Two, Six, Ten and Seven
and now there are eight Regiments instead of the eleven.

They fought in Singapore and Brunei, Borneo and Burma;
Afghanistan, the Falklands, Tobruk, and even further.
I heard it said: "The safest place is at a Gurkha's side
in warfare". In peacetime too I'm sure it's true this cannot be denied.

For five whole days, in a blissful haze, we enjoyed the celebrations
of K.E.O Goorkha Rifles, who are drawn from several regions.
All Gurkha Regiments are held in high renown*
but I sense the 'Second' Goorkhas is the jewel in the crown.

---

* *Having been witness to this historic and unique occasion, the words with which I would describe the Gurkhas are: camaraderie; commitment; courage in battle; discipline; grace; loyalty; true humility without arrogance; and, last but by no means least: mutual respect and friendship.*

HIMALAYAN HEAVEN at
TIGER MOUNTAIN POKHARA LODGE

Surely we took a voyage nearer heaven when we reached TMLP,
and as I sit here by the pool, there's nowhere I'd rather be.
It's like a private party, each one doing their own thing,
with Marcus, our most gracious host, attentive and charming.

The only trouble here is that it's so difficult to tell
whether 'tis a Brigadier - or Lieutenant Gen-er-al
sitting there beside one, quietly drinking in the scene -
or even a Field Marshall it might easily have been.

The Chappells and the Duffells, and the Thomases of course:
they'd all been inspirational in gath'ring the Simoors;
yet it was so kind of them to include us in their midst
within the Gurkha family, and made us feel at ease.

The staff were grand, right there at hand, always ready with a smile;
they all seemed absolutely willing to go the extra mile.
I say Hooray to be away from the U.K., pre-election,
especially in this glorious place, which to me is near perfection.

We saw some Himalayan haystacks, and woodpiles two a penny,
and some very simple homesteads, but there were not very many;
it was terraces, not palaces, that we did there espy
and the tilling of the land in true tranquillity.

We had sneak peeks of the mountain peaks when the sun dispersed the cloud,
but you had to be quick to catch these chinks, not always readily allowed.
I gazed around at the awesome sight, and basked in Nature's Glory:
how could one wonder or have doubts about Creation's story?

The mountains and the clouds took turns to fill our view,
like actors' entrances and exeunts - when it was their cue;
suddenly a shaft of light shone straight down from the sky:
it almost seemed that it was beamed - like torchlight from on high.

Hari took us on a mini trek - right away from all the throng;
oh! the beauty in these foothills and the melodious birdsong.
Who needs quadraphonic sound, with all those birds around?
It surely does one's soul some good to hear those clear sweet sounds.

It's going to be so difficult to tear ourselves away
from the ever-changing mountains and their dazzle-ing display.
To Machhapuchhre the Magnificent, a.k.a. Mount Fishtail,
and to Annapurna and Lamjung, soon we have to say Farewell.

To the bulbuls and great barbets, and the white-crested laughing thrush.
We heard them all, but to hear them call, we had to hush, not rush.
The long-beaked Crimson Sunbird; the minivet with yellow breast
and the green-billed Malcoha were among the rest.

Then Geoffrey went with Hari, to find Picus Squamatus:
that's the onomatopoeic name: scaly-bellied woodpecker it is known to us!
Of his ornithological knowledge one would simply never tire,
but now you'll have to be content with the Rhayader Male Voice Choir.

Thank you SO much, Geoffrey and Cornelia for including us in
your lovely group for one of the best holidays I have ever had.

MY EIGHTIETH BIRTHDAY

I can hardly believe that I have reached the advanced age of eighty, and I wanted to gather the whole family and spend a few days together. With my eldest daughter living in Hawai'i that is never possible, and sadly Isabel was in Argentina, and Claira had just started a new job. Simon cleverly collected Jamie and Rose from school, and I think we mustered about sixteen. We took a house in Herefordshire which fitted us in brilliantly, and it was a very happy time.

We loved the little steam train that chugged around the estate with us all aboard.

But the highlight for me was when they all got up to sing a wonderful ditty that Nick my son-in-law had written to the tune of Cwm Rhondda. It was the story of my life and I was so flabbergasted that I honestly didn't know whether to laugh - or cry tears of joy. Thank you SO much everybody - Nick it was brilliant. Here it is.

> Growing up near Bishop's Stortford, riding ponies every day,
> Peg and Peter's only daughter, John was with her all the way.
> Wanny, Wuffy, Buppy, Guggy all adored Penelope (Penelope).
> All adored Penelope.
>
> First the Barn School, later Paris, then to London with a splash.
> A few beaux suggested marriage, but she sailed on unattached.
> Eponino, Eponino. Uncle Dick would sing her name (sing her name).
> Uncle Dick would sing her name.

Off she went to stay near Brecon where she met a leading light:
Not what she thought or planned for, but she knew that it was right…
Enter Mervyn, enter Mervyn: he braved the Roller and the rest (and the rest).
Epony was heading west.

Soon Llwyn Madoc got more homely, and some mod cons arrived at last!
Tatti, Sarah, Patrick, Lucy - children popped out pretty fast.
Ponies, dogs and Mrs Davis - Mrs B made quite a home (quite a home).
Mrs B made quite a home.

Endless rides with all the Harleys, Keown-Boyds and many more.
Royal Welsh Show and lots of parties; there was endless fun in store.
Trips to Garrows, life in Beulah: Welsh cakes, roses, Sweep and Spade
(Sweep and Spade).
Welsh cakes, roses, Sweep and Spade.

A letter came in from the Palace asking Merv to be Lord-'Loot'
There evolved a life in lay-bys, straightening out both sword and suit.
Squiring royals, dancing farmers, pinning medals far and wide (far and wide).
Ep-ny always at his side.

Children grew up, and got married; new broods turned up fairly soon.
Allans, Bourdies, Mieses, Blancos loved Dare's upstairs jungle room.
Then to Gilwern in the summer and the
playground in the woods (in the woods).
'We survived the zipwire too'!

Now Dare winters up in Oxford, cooking bacon for the young.
Garden projects fill her summer, walls are built and gates are hung.
Dare is 80, Dare is 80 - What a grandmother,
great grandmother, (mother-in-law).
HAPPY BIRTHDAY from us all.

SO DARE IS 80 - WHY ALL THE FUSS?!

I have been so very fortunate and am still feeling quite elated
At the quite remarkable way that my birthday has been celebrated.

It all began last year when "Mrs B was not quite 80"
when we asked the folk in Beulah to come and help us party.

After Charlie's wedding, in the marquee upon the lawn
we took the opportunity to dine and dance, not quite, 'til dawn:

The Bourdillon gals were brilliant and got most people on the floor
and Heath and Tony's music kept us begging them for more.

Then in Oxford in the winter (Anne and) I shared a party in a pub
for Moyne's amazing Group: we enjoyed good comp'ny and good grub.

Next came the Pony Party at St. Dennis in the spring:
Thanks to the Mieses' generosity, and Luce had thought of everything.

Surely one would normally expect equines to live in stables,
but one of the sensations were blow up ponies on the tables.

'twas the happiest occasion: a triumphant trip down Memory Lane
with such **very** special friends, all so pleased to meet again.

COVID CHRISTMAS

I was going to spend this Christmas with th' Allans at Kentisbeare,
but with Coronavirus raging, it was not a good idea.
I was so very fortunate to be welcomed at St. Dennis,
Thus Covid 19, and what that might mean,
for me was really in no way a menace...

Jamie made cocktails with all the right things:
French Seventy Five was especially delicious;
not quite sure what it had in: it must have been gin,
though it made me a little suspicious!!
And Simon gave us fine wine which we couldn't decline,
along with the best of Champagne,
So we sat and we drank - and then drank some more,
then 'twas time to eat, yet again.

We ate meal after meal, and laughed a great deal,
and played some ridiculous games;
There was one, it was ace, with whipped cream in your face,
but I cannot remember its name.
Then we got whizzing and did some good quizzing,
but by then we were all a bit drunk;
but 'tween us all, in the light, we got a few right,
but I can't remember what we had 'thunk'.

Christmas Day off we went, and a great time was spent
taking food round to the old and the lonely
after Honington Church, where we were lucky to perch,
since they could take about thirty five only.
That evening we sped to the Pougatch(es) and played
some good games - and raced our own polar bears:
Commentating not lost, with kind Mark as our host,
and Cornelius also was there.

Claira went riding, but couldn't go hunting:
in any case her horse Dolly was lame;
and then she produced - helped a little by Luce -
'Beef Welly' that lived up to its name.
She and Harriet donned such glamorous clothes
that wowed us, when changing for dinner.
Hat's trousers were striking: black and gold - not for hiking -
and she could not have looked any trimmer.

She was busily working, 'cos her finals were lurking,
and her Dissertation had to be written.
We were all in a bubble which saved so much trouble,
though with masks we were not at all smitten.
Shopping with Jamie was nice; we found dear little mice -
Lucy's birthday was coming up soon.
Then we found my mobile, a strange story to tell,
and had lovely dog walks before noon.

Si took us away and we all spent the day
at the National Memorial Arb'retum;
we got a bit peckish, so bought chips and fish,
but were not quite sure where we could eat 'em…
and, ho! ho! ho! ho! it tried hard to snow,
but Jamie drove us exceedingly well.
It was a great outing, so very exciting,
and we all gave our vote: 'It was swell'.

And who made it all happen, with much preparation
but Lucy, who fed us: Hooray!
She gave us all stockings and never stopped working
to make sure we were happy all day.
So thank you dear things (for) taking me under your wings,
I might have been all on my own here.
We didn't need sherry to make us all merry;
so thanks to you **all**, and much love from Dare.

WHAT A PAIR!

I am so proud of my grandchildren in many and various ways. It was exciting to hear last summer that Harriet had got a First in English at Edinburgh, and then we had to wait a week before Flora heard her results. The two cousins are very close friends so it was a great relief and delight to hear that she had also got a First - in Clinical Psychology, at Exeter. I wrote these ridiculous lines to them both:

> I am glad you got the grade that you so obviously deserved;
> That's why I'm sending you this profound congratulation.
> Your Course was jolly hard, but from which you never swerved –
> With all those dreadful sounding words - quite beyond my education!
>
> I have a sort of inkling
> that glasses might be tinkling
> and toes should be a-twinkling
> in Exeter and Edinburgh.
>
> And another sort of feeling
> a few hearts might need a-healing,
> but I hope there's lots of reeling
> in Edinburgh, if not in Exeter.

For Harriet
Worth all your hard work to get the extra points that you were needing:
at least three books a day and all that Christmas reading.

For Flora
I am so very proud of you: that's the very least that I can say
and now you have another year which will take you further on your way.

I wish you both many blessings on the next stage of your journey.

CHRISTMAS IN DEVON

A is for Anna the Wizard of Inst.
Also for Ada who arrived in our midst.
B is for Books, read and written right here.
C is for Cate and much Christmas Cheer.
D is for dogs, always wanting a walk.
E is for Epony who drank all that port.
F is for Family, Fun and good Food.
G is for Grub when we felt in the mood.
H is for Helena; was her dissertation causing her strife?
I is for Instagram - (which might become the bane of my life!)
J is for Jonny - released at last from isolation.
Kentisbeare was filled with joy and jubilation;
Lexi blew in, but no Keith sad to tell, and
Matilda was not feeling too well.
Nick was not only our generous host:
Oh! he certainly was the host with the most.
Presents galore were all over the floor.
Queues were not needed outside the church door.
R is for Reindeer, Robins and Rain.
S is for Sarah who fed us again and again;
Thank you for giving us such a nice time.
T is for Turkey, with Trimmings sublime;
V is for Vegans (not really my line!)
Walks round the garden in rain and sunshine.
Xmas is not a good word - I rather prefer
Yuletide - how about you? and
Zat is just about all you can stand!

Lightning Source UK Ltd.
Milton Keynes UK
UKHW010919160522
403010UK00001B/5